Magnets

Originally published as

Junior Science Book of Magnets

By

Rocco V. Feravolo

Illustrated by

Evelyn Urbanowich

Living Library Press
PO Box 16141
Bristol, Virginia 24201

All About Magnets was originally published in 1960 by Garrard Publishing Company. The dedication page to *All About Magnets* has the following statement:

> Junior Science Books are dedicated to all children who are eager to know more about nature and the world they live in. Written especially for young readers, each Junior Science Book has been carefully tested by the Spache Readability Formula. The purpose of this evaluation is to assure that each book can be read by primary grade children and enjoyed by young readers through the elementary grades.
>
> Junior Science Books are edited and designed under the educational supervision of Nancy Larrick, Ed.D.

The current edition has been revised and updated by Living Library Press. All rights are reserved and no part of this book may be reproduced without written permission from Living Library Press.

ISBN #: 978-0-692-83664-4

©2017 Living Library Press
P.O. Box 16141
Bristol, VA 24201

Contents

1.	Magnets Attract	5
2.	Even Through Glass	11
3.	Why Magnets Attract	16
4.	Magnets Push, Too	21
5.	Magnetism Rubs Off	25
6.	A Needle Magnet	29
7.	How a Compass Works	33
8.	Floating in Air	42
9.	Magnets at Work	47
10.	Magnets and Electricity	57
	Index	63

1

Magnets Attract

Magnets have a strange power. They attract things of iron or steel. They seem to work like magic.

Hold a magnet near a pin, but not touching it. The pin jumps to the magnet and clings to it. Even when you lift the magnet, the pin hangs on. Try a nail. The same thing happens. We say the magnet attracts the steel pin or the iron nail.

Magnets are made in hundreds of shapes and sizes. The kind we see most often is shaped like a horseshoe. As you might guess, it is called a horseshoe magnet. You can buy one in a hardware store or in a toy shop.

Another kind of magnet is the bar magnet. It looks like this:

Magnets make interesting toys. But they do a great deal of work in houses and offices and factories. They make telephones work and doorbells ring. They pick up huge pieces of iron and steel. They even help to make electricity.

To learn how a magnet works, test it with different things. Hold it close to a button on your coat. Nothing happens. Hold it over a piece of paper. The paper won't move. See if you can pick up a penny or a nickel or a dime. The coins will stay on the table.

Now try the magnet with a paper clip. Watch it jump!

Slide your magnet very slowly across the table toward the paper clip. Notice how far it jumps. A strong magnet will pull a paper clip more than an inch away.

You can experiment with dozens of

different things. Get two large cardboard boxes. Label one box WILL ATTRACT and label the other WILL NOT ATTRACT. Then start testing with paper clips, keys, pencils, scissors, screws, tinfoil, glass, and anything else you find. Everything that sticks to the magnet goes into the WILL ATTRACT box. Everything else goes into the WILL NOT ATTRACT box.

Take a careful look at all the things that went into the WILL ATTRACT box. You will see that each of them is made of iron or steel, or is partly iron or steel. Magnets always attract iron or steel. They won't attract copper, lead, gold, silver, aluminum, brass, zinc, or most other metals. They won't attract glass or wood or plastics.

A magnet can sometimes be a detective. It can tell you what things really are. You know that a magnet won't pull anything made of copper. Take a paper clip that looks like copper and watch it jump to the magnet. This is because the paper clip isn't really copper. It is steel, colored like copper. A magnet attracts steel.

Try your magnet on the hinges of a door. They are the color of brass. A magnet doesn't attract brass. If it sticks, you know the hinges aren't solid brass. They are steel with a thin coating of brass.

Try your magnet on a house key that is the color of steel. It probably won't stick. House keys are usually made of soft metals, not iron or steel.

2

Even Through Glass

A cat can smell fish through several pieces of paper. A magnet can attract metal through several dozen sheets of paper—or even through glass.

Put a paper clip on a table and hold a sheet of paper over it. Put the magnet against the top of the paper. The paper clip will jump up.

Now use a thin magazine or booklet. If your magnet is strong enough, it will attract a paper clip underneath.

Put your magnet next to the paper label on a tin can. The magnet sticks to the paper. That is because the can is really made of thin steel, with a coating of tin over it. The magnet pulls through the paper and tin because of the steel inside.

Put a few nails in an empty glass jar. Move your magnet up and down on the outside. The nails will move up and down, too. The pull of the magnet goes through glass.

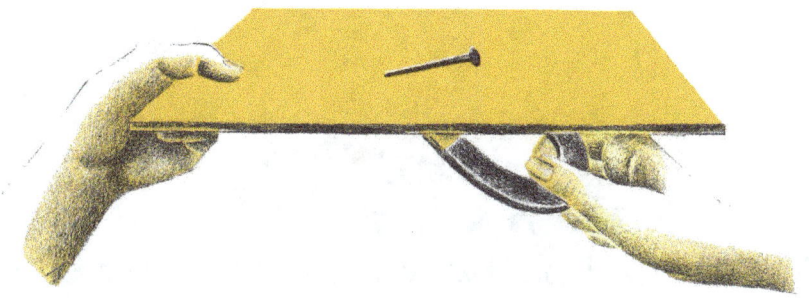

A magnet will also pull through a thin piece of wood. Find some plywood or the side of a box about one quarter inch thick. Put a nail or paper clip on top. Move the magnet around underneath, and the nail will move too. But if the wood is a thick board, the magnet can't pull through it.

You can make a toy boat that runs by magnetic power. First, make a boat about three inches long out of a small block of

wood. Fasten a nail on the bottom with tacks.

Drive a nail partway into the other side for a mast. Be careful not to split the wood. Put a piece of paper over the nail to make a sail.

Get a large aluminum pie plate or aluminum baking dish for your lake. It won't be damaged. The pie plate should be a few inches above the table so you can get your hand beneath it. You can rest it on tin cans or a wire stand from a coat hanger. Twist the coat hanger so it has three legs.

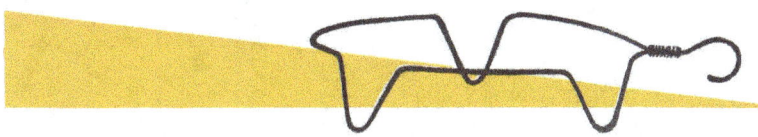

Put the pie plate on the stand and fill it with water. Set your boat in the water. Hold the magnet under the pie plate and move it around. You have a mystery boat. It moves wherever you guide it.

Of course there's an answer to the mystery. It's the nail on the bottom of the boat. The magnet pulls through the plate and the water to the nail. The iron nail is attracted to the magnet.

3

Why a Magnet Attracts

Nobody knows why a magnet attracts things.

Most scientists think the secret is in the way iron is made. Iron looks hard and solid. But it is really made of millions and millions of moving bits called molecules. They are much too small to see with your eye. But we know that they are moving all the time. Each molecule is a tiny magnet by itself. If the molecules are scattered every which way, they all pull in different directions. There is no magnetic force then.

Think of four people pulling in different directions on two ropes tied in the middle.

Nobody moves. The force of each one is wasted. But if you line up the four people to pull in the same direction, you have a strong force.

Probably the same thing happens with the molecules in iron. In a magnet, the iron molecules are lined up. They all pull in the same direction. That is magnetic force.

A magnet always pulls hardest at the two ends, called the poles. Your horseshoe magnet won't pull up anything much at the top. A bar magnet won't attract things to its center.

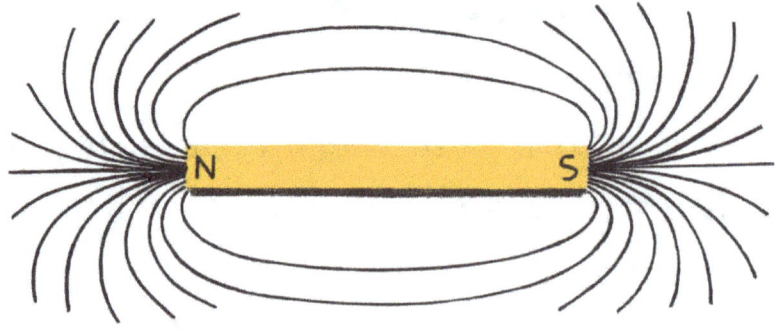

You can see how much the poles pull if you get some iron filings from a machine shop, or from a hole made in iron by an electric drill. Lay a piece of paper over a bar magnet. Scatter some iron filings on the paper.

Now tap the paper gently. The iron filings will gather at the ends of the magnet. They will go to the poles.

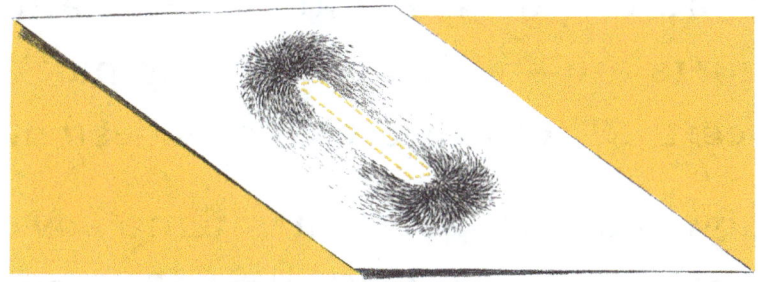

Try the same experiment with a horseshoe magnet. Again the iron filings will be drawn to the poles.

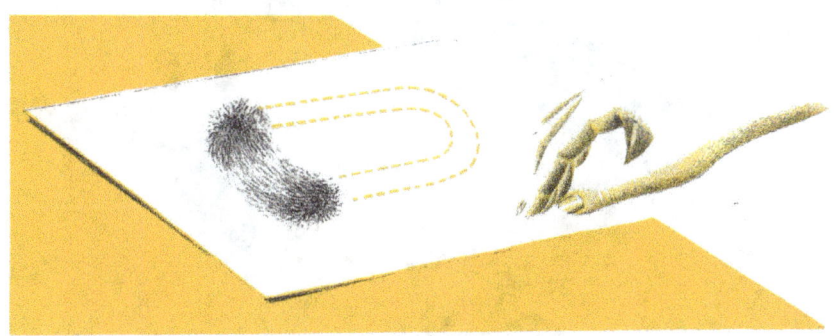

If you could cut a bar magnet in half, each piece would have two poles, too. Every magnet has two poles.

The first magnets were discovered more than 2,000 years ago. They were a kind of iron ore called magnetite. These natural magnets are still found in many parts of the earth. They are known as lodestones.

How did they get their pulling power? Probably from the earth itself. The earth has its own magnetism. It is the biggest magnet we know anything about.

4

Magnets Push, Too

We generally think of magnets as pulling. But they can also push. This happens when two magnets come together in a certain way. To see how they push, you need two bar magnets.

On one end of a bar magnet you will find the letter N. N stands for North. N marks the North pole of the magnet. Take a soft pencil or crayon and print S on the other end of both magnets. That means South pole.

Build a wooden stand to look like this:

Or you can use the bottom rung of a wooden chair.

Tie a strong cotton or silk thread around one bar magnet and hang it from the stand or chair rung. Be sure the magnet can swing freely in any direction.

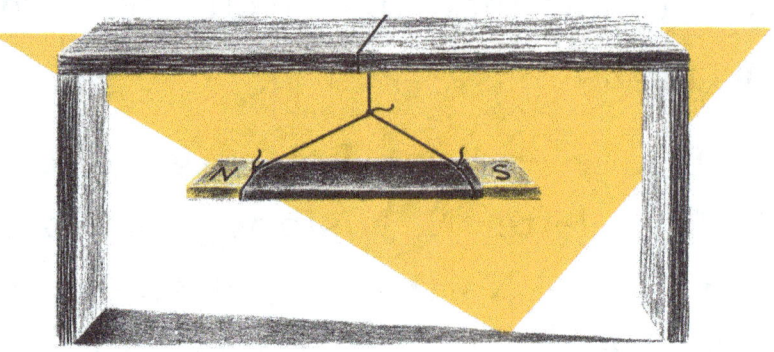

Hold the other bar magnet so the N pole is close to the N pole of the swinging magnet. The magnet in your hand will push the other magnet away without touching it.

Next, put the two S poles close together. Again the magnet you are holding will push back the swinging magnet.

Now put the S pole of one magnet near the N pole of the other. The two magnets come together like long lost friends.

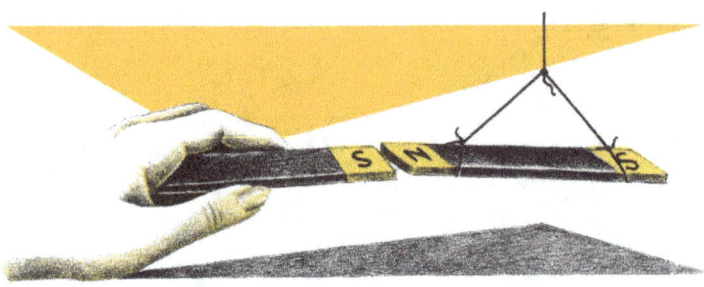

It's always the same with magnets. Poles that are the same push away from each other. Poles that are different attract each other.

5

Magnetism Rubs Off

The power of a magnet will travel through things made of iron or steel.

You can see for yourself. Pick up a paper clip with your magnet. Now touch the hanging paper clip to another one. The second one clings to the first. Probably you can make a chain of three or four paper clips.

You can make a small magnet out of a nail.

Hold a good sized nail in one hand. With a bar magnet rub the nail from the middle to the pointed end. Either end of the magnet will work provided you always use the same end. Rub very slowly, about 20 or 30 times.

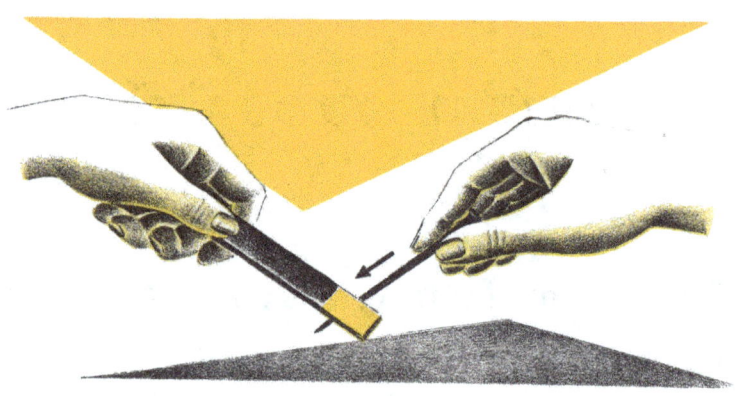

Be careful to rub the nail in only one direction, toward the point. Move the magnet away from the nail after each stroke.

Try to pick up a pin with the nail. The nail should work like a magnet. If it won't

pick up the pin, stroke it some more with the bar magnet. Then the nail will pick up two or three pins.

You can also take the magnetism out of the nail. Fill a pan with cold water and put it on the gas range. Light the burner next to the pan. Take a pair of pliers and pick up the nail. Hold the nail over the flame for about three minutes, until it glows red hot.

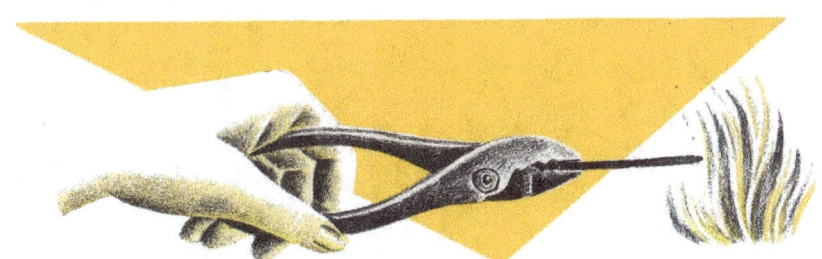

Now drop the nail into the pan of cold water. It will sizzle for a moment. You can take it out with your fingers. Try to pick up a pin. The pin won't move. The nail isn't a magnet any more.

Why does heat take the magnetism out of the nail? You remember that iron or steel is magnetic when the tiny molecules are lined up, like soldiers on parade. Heat makes the molecules jump around. You would move, too, if you touched the hot nail. When the molecules jump around, they pull in many different directions. The magnetism is gone.

6

A Needle Magnet

Get a long steel darning needle. Rub it slowly with one end of a bar magnet. Rub it toward the point about 30 times, as you rubbed the nail. Remember to lift up your magnet after each stroke.

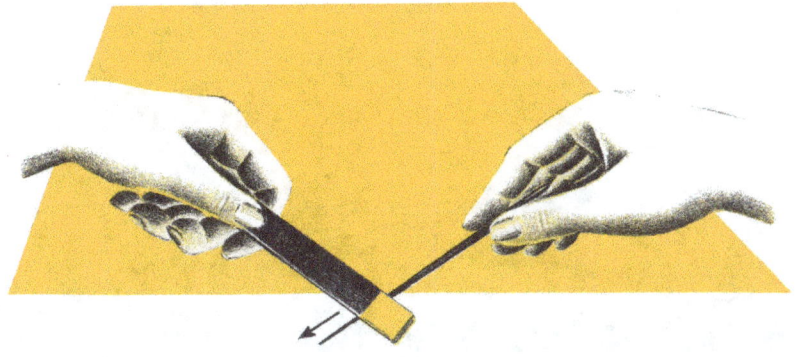

You will have a magnetic needle. It will pick up pins.

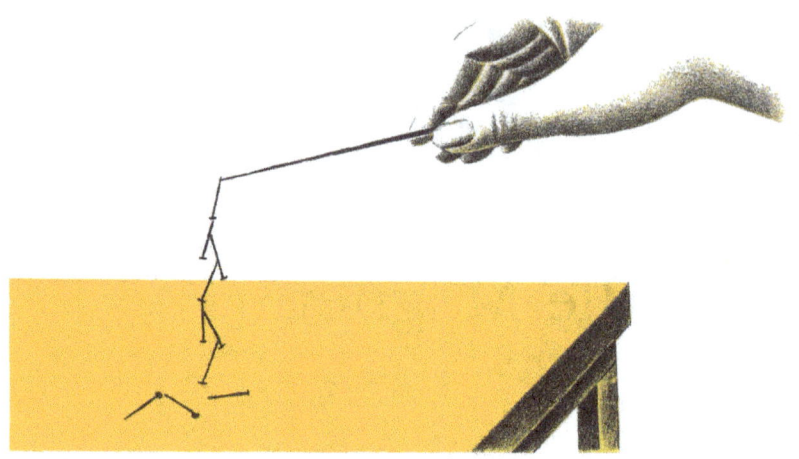

In fact, your needle magnet is even stronger than a nail magnet. Count how many pins each magnet will pick up.

A needle magnet will do more than pick up pins. Push the needle through a cork, like this:

Fill an aluminum pie plate with water and float the needle magnet. The needle will point to the North. Twist the cork to make the needle point in another direction. The cork will turn back so the needle points North again. You can keep

twisting all day long—but the needle will always swing North when you take your fingers away.

Your needle is more than a magnet. It's a compass. It tells you where the North is.

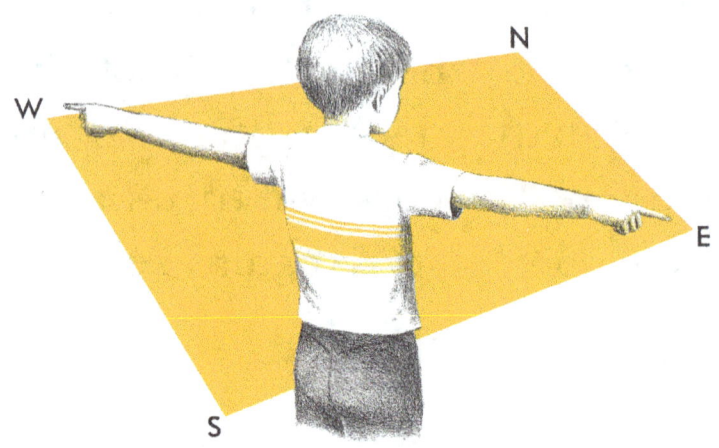

If you know where North is, you know the other directions, too. Stand up and face the North. The South is behind you. Your right hand is East and your left hand is West.

This is a handy thing to remember when you find your way among the streets of a big city. Or the trees of a big woods.

7

How a Compass Works

A pocket compass is worth having. You can probably buy one at a sporting goods store in the camping section. Or you can order one online, through Amazon.com or any other camping outfitter. Prices vary from around $6.00 and go up to over $100.00. There are many to choose from but they all operate the same way.

Look at the face of your compass.

You know that N stands for North and S is for South. E is for East, where the sun rises. W is for West, where the sun sets. In between N, E, S, and W are the two-letter directions. NE means Northeast, just halfway between North and East. SE is for Southeast, halfway between South and East.

The different sections of the United States are called by the same names. The United States has an East and West, a North and a South. Part of the East is the Northeast, and part is the Southeast. And so for the rest of the country.

The most interesting part of your compass is the needle. It moves. Actually the needle is a small magnet. It always points North, just like the needle magnet in the pie plate.

Turn the compass in different directions. The needle moves so it keeps pointing North. Magnetism in the earth itself pulls the needle toward the North.

The way to use a compass is to hold it

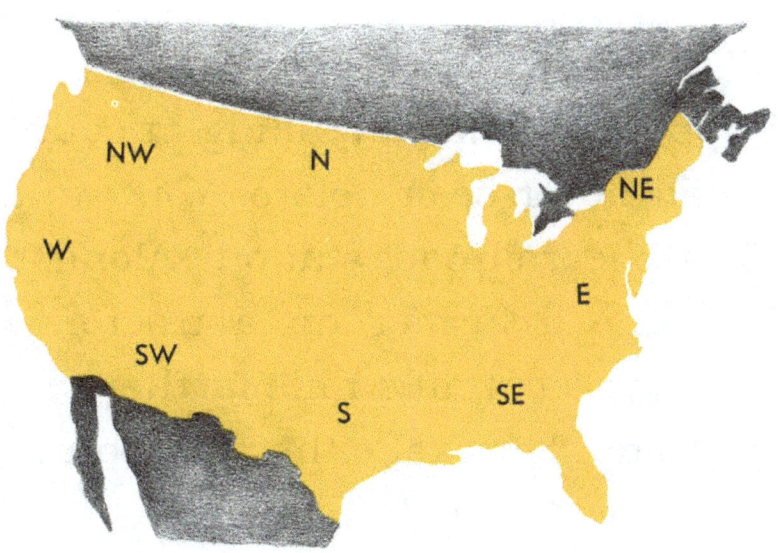

so the point of the needle is over the letter N. Then the other directions will be where the compass shows them. South will be right behind you, East at your right, West at your left.

Suppose you were walking in country you had never seen before. You wanted to find the railroad station. Along the road came a farmer on a tractor. He might say: "Go half a mile farther to the crossroads. Then take the road South. It goes to the station."

If you had a compass, you could follow his directions. You would hold the compass with the needle over the N. Then you would walk the other way, to the South.

Hundreds of years ago there were no compasses. The captains of sailing ships watched the sun and the North Star. Then they could tell whether they were sailing North or South, East or West.

But on cloudy days and nights there was no sun to guide them and no North Star. A ship far out at sea could get lost. So captains tried to keep within sight of land. A coastline is never straight. Following the coast made ships go zig-zag instead of straight. Voyages were much longer.

Look at a map of North and South America. Imagine a ship following the land from New York to Rio de Janeiro. Rio de Janeiro is actually southeast of New York. But the ship would have to travel South and North and West and East and South. It would go thousands of extra miles. It would sale past Mexico, Venezuela, and many other countries before it reached Brazil.

With a compass, a ship can go directly to Rio de Janeiro. The captain looks at

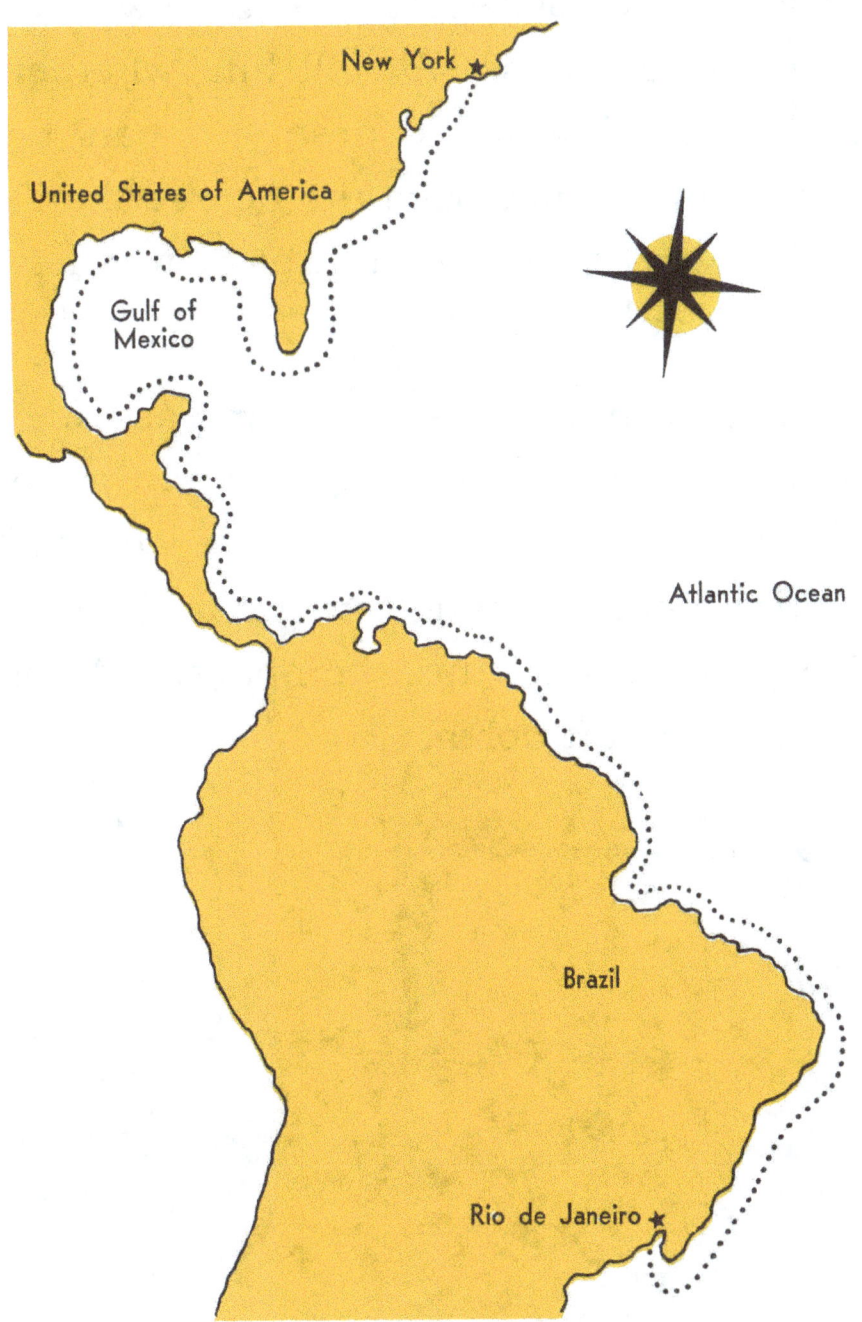

a map. He decides what his course will be. Then the compass will tell him whether he is following his course. He can be hundreds of miles from the nearest land. But he won't get lost so long as he watches his compass.

For the fun of it, put your compass on a table. Hang your bar magnet by a thread from its stand. Put the pie plate with the floating needle magnet on the table, too. Now you will have three compasses. All of them will point north.

Move your real compass close to the bar magnet. Watch the needle. The bar magnet will turn it away from the North.

That's because the bar magnet is pulling the needle harder than the earth does at this point. But if you move the magnet away, the needle will swing back to the North. That's where the earth's magnetism has a pole.

Iron objects close to a compass will move the needle, too. The needle is always attracted by iron.

8

Floating in Air

Magnets can do many things that seem impossible. You can use a magnet to make a paper clip float in air.

For this experiment you will need a wooden stand. Get a two-foot piece of wood, either 1 x 4 or 1 x 6. Cut two blocks six inches long. Then nail the long piece to them.

Now set the stand on end. Drive a big

tack or a small nail partway into the lower piece of the stand.

Put your bar magnet on top of the stand so it sticks out. Tie a piece of string to a paper clip. Let the paper clip touch the magnet. The magnet will hold it. Now wrap the other end of the string around the tack. Wind it slowly to make

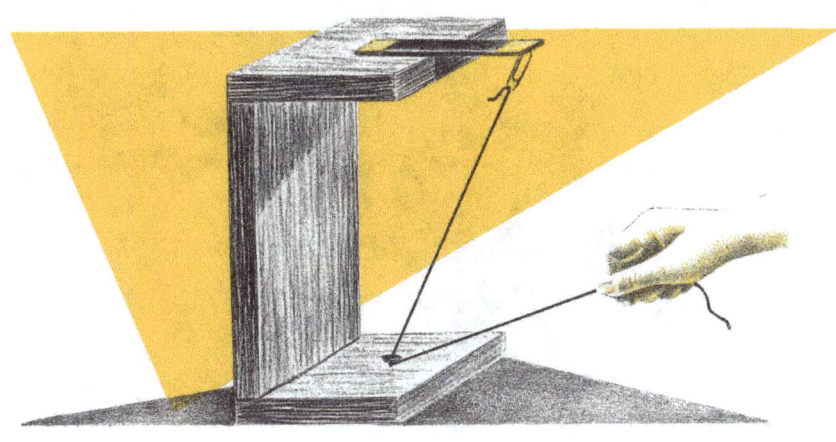

the string shorter. Stop winding when you pull the paper clip away from the magnet. Now the paper clip will float in air.

The magnet attracts the clip. But the string keeps the clip from touching the magnet. It's like a cat coming near a dog

on a chain. The cat attracts the dog. But the dog can't get to it. The chain stops him.

You can make a bar magnet float in air, too. For this experiment you need a block of wood about 3 x 6 inches, although a larger block will do just as well. You also need two bar magnets and four nails. The magnets must be strong but not heavy.

Put one bar magnet on the block and mark a line around it with a pencil. Hammer four nails partway into the wood, like this:

Now put one bar magnet between the nails. Put another bar magnet on top of it. Be sure that the North pole of the top magnet is over the North pole of the other.

The top magnet will actually float above the other magnet. That's because the same poles always push away from each other.

Pick up the top magnet and turn it around. Put it back with the South pole over the North pole of the bottom magnet. Now the two magnets stick together. Unlike poles always attract.

9

Magnets At Work

Magnets are a big help to men who work in machine shops and garages. Every now and then a nut or some other small metal part will drop from a wrench or from a man's hand. Sometimes it falls where it can't be reached with fingers or pliers. It may be in the machinery itself. The machinery could get broken if the lost nut stayed in it.

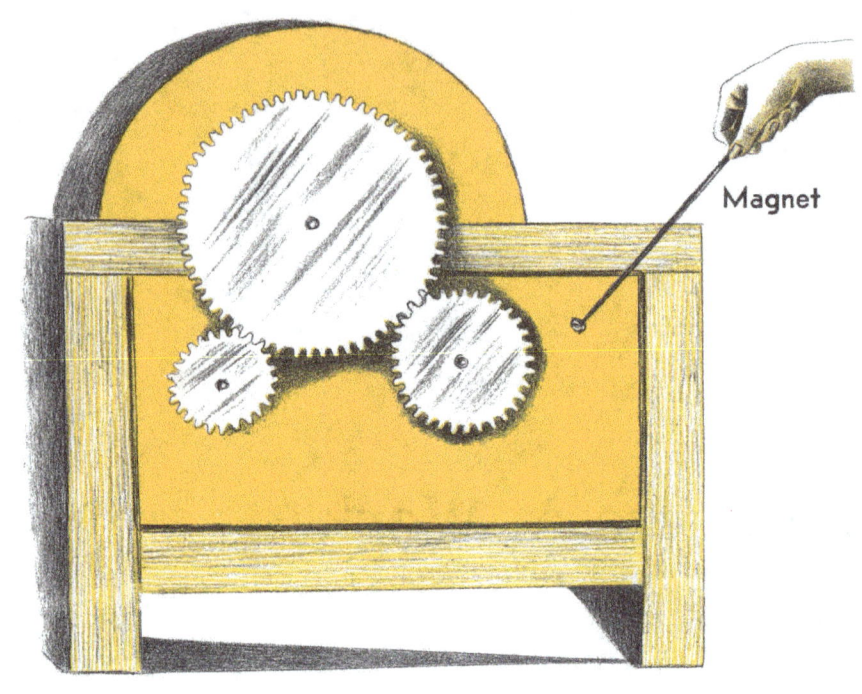

So the mechanic goes fishing. He doesn't use a fishing line with a hook. Instead he takes a long slender rod. The rod is a magnet. As soon as the end of the rod gets close to the nut, the nut jumps to the magnet. The mechanic lifts the nut out and the fishing is over. Time and money are saved.

Magnets in machine shops are stronger

than toy magnets. But they can't lift very heavy things. For big jobs, electromagnets are used. An electromagnet gets its power from electricity. You can make a small electromagnet with a big nail, about three feet of doorbell wire, and a dry cell. You can get these at a hardware store.

Leave a foot of wire free. Then make about 20 tight turns around the nail, like this:

Now scrape off the insulation for about an inch at each end of the wire. Loosen the brass screws on the two terminals of the dry cell. Wrap the bare wire around the terminals. Tighten the screws. You now have an electromagnet that will pick up pins.

The magnet gets its power from electricity in the dry cell. The current flowing around and around the nail makes what is called a magnetic field. This magnetic field attracts iron as a regular magnet does.

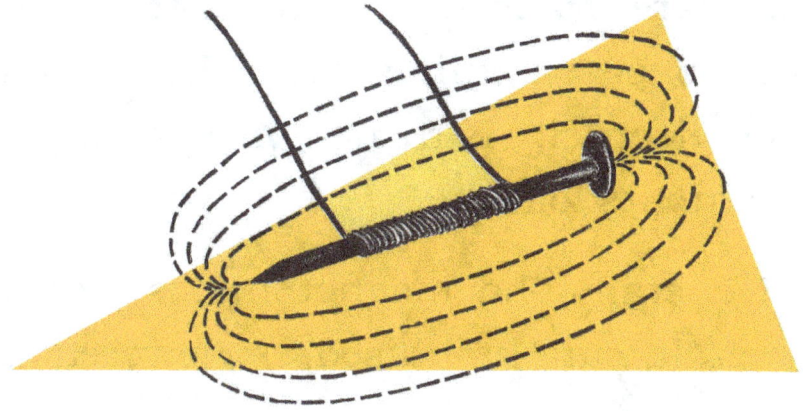

If you take either wire away from the dry cell, the electromagnet stops working. The magnetic field is gone. Electricity has to flow in a circuit to make an electromagnet.

If you leave your wires connected too long, the dry cell will go dead like a worn out flashlight battery.

At steel mills and big junkyards, electromagnets are used to lift heavy pieces of iron. These electromagnets don't look like the one you made with a nail and wire. But they work the same way. Coils of wire are wrapped around a piece of iron that looks something like a huge cake. When electricity is turned on, the magnet picks up its load.

Generally the magnet hangs from a crane. It can be raised or lowered by

steel cables. Sometimes the crane has a caterpillar tread like an army tank. It can move around the yard, carrying its load. Or the crane may travel on steel rails, like a locomotive.

When the crane operator wants to drop his load of iron or steel, he turns off the

electricity. This breaks the magnetic field. There is no magnet when the current is off.

An electromagnet saves a lot of time. Without an electromagnet, men would have to fasten steel cables around the iron. Then they would have to unfasten the cables to dump the load.

The nineteenth-century French magician, Jean-Eugene Robert-Houdin, used an electromagnet in one of his famous tricks. He built a wooden box with an iron bottom. He put it on the stage just above a powerful electromagnet. Then he would ask a strong man in the audience to lift the box. The man could do it easily. "Now I will make you weak," Houdin would say. A helper, out of sight, would then turn on the electricity. "Now try to lift the box," the magician said next.

Try as he might, the strong man couldn't pull the box away from the electromagnet.

Magnets are used in many kitchens today to hold cupboard doors shut. A small magnet about an inch long is screwed underneath a shelf, at the edge. Then a thin metal plate is fastened to the door so it can touch the magnet. The door will pull open easily. It shuts easily, too. The magnet holds it in place.

Once more than 200 automobiles got flat tires on a highway in Indiana. A truck had been piled high with sharp steel shavings. As the truck jiggled along, the shavings jiggled off—for 22 miles. The shavings cut through tires like knives.

Two police cars went after the truck. They got flat tires, too. Finally the police sent for a truck carrying a crane. The crane had a powerful electromagnet. With the electromagnet out front, the truck went down the highway. All the steel shavings were picked up.

10

Magnets and Electricity

The great English scientist, Michael Faraday, made an important discovery in 1831. He found a way to make an electric current flow. All he did was to move a loop of wire in a magnetic field.

There was no electric current in the wire before it came near the magnet. But moving the wire in the space around the magnet made a current flow. Faraday proved this with tests.

Thomas Edison and other inventors kept experimenting with electricity. How could they use Faraday's discovery to make strong electric currents?

Finally they built a machine to make electricity flow. The kind of machine they built is still being used today. It is called a generator, or dynamo.

The generator has many coils of wire on a wheel. The wheel is turned at a terrific speed by water power or steam

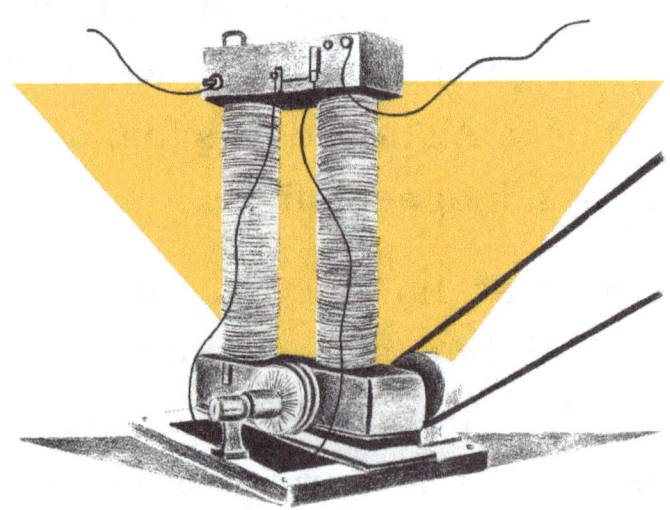

power. As it turns, the coils of wire pass by a series of magnets.

The wires on the electric wheel become charged with an electric current.

The machine in the picture is a generator, or dynamo. The huge dynamos in powerhouses are much more complicated. They turn at terrific speeds. The electric current goes from the powerhouse through wires and cables to houses, stores, factories, and many other places.

Electricity is needed to make electric motors turn. An electric motor is something like a generator. But it works in the opposite way. Instead of making an electric current, it uses electricity. The electricity going into the motor makes the wheel turn. Magnetic force keeps the wheel turning.

The wheel is fastened to an axle. The

axle turns, too. It will turn the wheels of any kind of machine. For example, an electric fan is turned in this way.

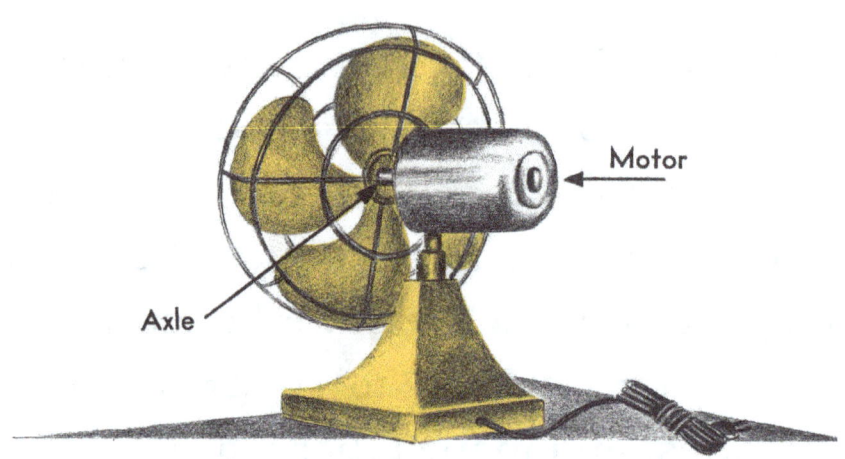

Electric motors are used in thousands of ways. They run locomotives. They run miniature trains, too, with magnets. They run ships. They lift bridges and elevators and the windows of automobiles.

All kinds of machines in factories are run with electric motors.

Motors go into the sky in airplanes. The pilot of a big passenger plane could not raise the wing flaps by hand. He could not turn the rudder by hand. He could not raise the landing gear by hand when he takes off. Electric motors with magnets do these jobs.

Magnets are now traveling in outer space. Rockets and satellites need electricity for fuel pumps and radios and other equipment. They carry generators to make their own electricity. Magnets make the generators work.

Magnets have changed our lives. Today we can hardly imagine a world without them.

Index

Compass, 31-32
Crane, 52-54

Dry cell, 49-51
Dynamo, 58-59

Earth as a magnet, 20, 25, 41
Electric motors, 59-61
Electromagnet, 49-54, 56

Faraday, Michael, 57

Generator, 58-59. 61

Highway accident, 56
Houdin, Robert, 54

Iron filings, 18-19

Lodestones, 20

Magic with a magnet, 54-55
Magnetic boat, 13-15
Magnetic door catch, 55
Magnetic field, 51, 54, 57
Magnetic force, 18, 59
Magnetism, 25-28
Magnetite, 20

Magnets
  Attract steel and iron, 5, 8-9, 12
  Attract through paper, glass, wood, 11-12, 13
  Discovery, 20
  Floating magnet, 42-46
  Making a magnet, 25-28, 29
  Pushing power, 21, 46
  Shapes of magnets, 6
  Space travel, 61
  Testing with magnets, 7-10
  Work of magnets, 7, 9, 47-49, 52-53, 55, 56
Molecules, 16-18, 28

Navigation, 37-40
Needle magnet, 29-31
New York, 38
North Star, 37, 38

Poles of a magnet, 18-20, 21-24, 46

Rio de Janeiro, 38
Sun, 37, 38

Testing with magnets, 7-10